Tiffany and Max Solve a Mystery

I Talk You Talk Press

CONTENTS

CHAPTER ONE

Max Lambert is in the university café. He is waiting for his girlfriend. Her name is Tiffany, but Max always calls her Tiff. Max is a student. He's studying computer science. He's very smart. Tiffany is also a university student.

Where's Tiff? he thinks. *She's late. I have a class in twenty minutes. I hope she comes soon.*

Max's phone rings. *Maybe Tiff is calling me.* He looks at his phone. *No. It's my mother. Why does she want to talk to me?* He answers his phone.

"Hi Mom," says Max.

"Max! Max! You must come to dinner tonight!" His mother sounds very excited.

"But it's Tuesday. We always have family dinner on Sunday," says Max.

"Yes. I know. But please come tonight. Owen has wonderful news. Bring Tiffany. Come at six thirty pm. Don't be late."

His mother hangs up. Max looks at his phone.

Tiffany runs into the café. "Sorry I'm late. The teacher talked and talked and talked."

"It's OK," smiles Max. "I have to go soon, but are you free tonight?"

"Yes," says Tiffany. "Why?"

"My mother called. She said, 'Please come here tonight. Owen has wonderful news. Bring Tiffany. Come at six thirty pm'".

"What kind of news?" asks Tiffany.

"I don't know. But my mother was very excited. I'll come to your apartment at six o'clock." Max looks at his phone. "I have to go now. See you tonight."

CHAPTER TWO

That evening, Max rides his bicycle to Tiffany's apartment. She is waiting outside for him. Tiffany takes her bicycle from the bicycle shed and they ride to Max's parents' house.

When they walk inside, Max is very surprised. There is a bottle of champagne and candles on the table. Max's mother is smiling. She is wearing a party dress. Max's father is there too. He is wearing jeans and a T-shirt.

"Come in! Come in!" shouts Max's mother. "I'm so excited!"

Tiffany and Max see Owen. He's smiling too. There's a young dark-haired woman standing next to him.

Mrs Lambert pours champagne for everyone.

"Now Owen," she says. "Tell Max and Tiffany your wonderful news!"

Owen's face is red. "First," he says. "This is my girlfriend, Marissa. Marissa. Please meet my brother Max, and Tiffany."

Tiffany and Max say "Hi, Marissa. Nice to meet you."

Then Max asks, "So what is the wonderful news?"

"I got a new job. It's a very good job. It's in Hawaii."

"That's great!" says Max. "Well done!"

"Thank you," says Owen. "But I don't want to go to Hawaii without Marissa. So I asked Marissa to marry me, and she said 'yes'!"

Mrs Lambert starts talking. "We're going to have a wedding! I'm so excited! Owen must start his job in Hawaii in four weeks. Marissa and Owen will get married before they go. We have very little time to plan the wedding. Drink your champagne," she shouts. "We have a lot of planning to do."

Mr Lambert says, "Why don't we all sit down?"

"Where will you get married?" asks Tiffany.

"In this town," says Marissa. "I come from San Francisco. There is only a little time. So the wedding will be here."

"We will decide everything tonight!" says Mrs Lambert. "I have made a list."

She takes out a long list.

"It will be nice to have the wedding at Honeysuckle – they do lovely weddings. We have to pick a date and a time and contact them. We will ask 'Can you do the wedding on that day and at that time?' Honeysuckle will want to know the number of guests," says Mrs Lambert.

"Can you make a list?" she asks Marissa.

"My mother will come," says Marissa. "No one else. But please invite as many people as you like."

Mr Lambert drinks his glass of champagne very quickly. "Alicia," he says to his wife. "Are we going to eat dinner tonight? Are you going to cook?"

"Oh, Don," says Mrs Lambert. "Everything is in the kitchen, but I am too excited to think about food."

Max stands up. "It's OK, Mom," he says. "Tiff and I will cook."

Tiffany and Max go to the kitchen.

CHAPTER THREE

Max looks in the refrigerator. There are lamb chops. He takes them out. He finds salad greens and tomatoes.

"I guess we can cook the lamb chops and make a salad," he says. "We will need potatoes. I don't know why, but Dad is not happy. He likes potatoes, so let's make him happy."

Tiffany starts peeling potatoes, and Max washes the salad greens. The door to the dining room is open, so they can hear everything.

"Bridesmaids," says Mrs Lambert. "How many bridesmaids will you have?"

"I don't have any friends in this town," says Marissa. "So I won't have any bridesmaids."

"You must have a bridesmaid!" says Mrs Lambert. "Do you have any sisters or cousins?"

"They won't come to the wedding," says Marissa.

"How about someone from your office?" asks Mrs Lambert.

"No. I don't like the women I work with."

"Oh," says Mrs Lambert. "Well how about Tiffany? I'm sure Tiffany will say 'Yes' if you ask her to be your bridesmaid."

"Oh no!" shouts Marissa. "She is too pretty. Everyone will look at her. It's my wedding. I want everyone to look at me."

"I understand. We will ask our niece, Tonia. She's a very nice girl. She will be perfect."

Max hurries to the door and closes it. He looks at Tiffany. "Are you OK?"

"Of course I am," says Tiffany. "I never want to be a bridesmaid.

The bride always chooses very bad dresses."

Tiffany and Max sit down at the table and laugh. "Sorry Tiff. It's a good thing you don't want to be a bridesmaid. No one will want you! You are too pretty!"

"But who is Tonia?" asks Tiffany.

"Tonia is Dad's sister's daughter. She's a very nice person. I like her a lot. But I guess Mom thinks she is not as pretty as Marissa."

"I think that's rude!" says Tiffany.

"Well Marissa was rude about you!" answers Max.

"But I don't care!" shouts Tiffany.

Max doesn't say anything. Tiffany is very small. She has blonde hair and big blue eyes. She is very, very pretty. When she was young, her schoolmates called her 'Barbie'. Tiffany is very clever and kind, Tiffany gets angry because people often treat her like a cute little girl.

"Let's finish cooking dinner," he says.

The food is almost ready when the door opens, and Owen comes into the kitchen. "It's crazy out there," he says. "I want to go to the Town Office to get married, and then have a family dinner in a restaurant. But Marissa and Mom are talking about an orchestra and dancing.

"Marissa and Mom are going to the bride shop on Main Street tomorrow to look at dresses for Marissa and Tonia."

"Has anyone asked Tonia if she wants to be Marissa's bridesmaid?" asks Max.

"No," says Owen. "Maybe she will say 'no'. But I have a question for you. Will you be my best man?"

Max smiles at his brother. "Of course. Do I have to wear a suit?"

Owen looks at Max. Max is very tall and thin. He has red-brown hair. His hair is always untidy. He always wears jeans and old T-shirts. Owen laughs. "Maybe a tuxedo?"

"Oh no!" shouts Max.

Owen helps Tiffany and Max take the food to the dining room.

Everyone enjoys the meal. Don eats many potatoes. He smiles. "Thank you for the great meal," he says. "Max and Tiffany did all the cooking, so I will wash the dishes."

"Oh no," says Max. "Tiff and I will help you."

"So will I." Owen jumps up from his chair.

"No, Owen," says Alicia. "You will stay here. You will help Marissa and me plan the wedding."

In the kitchen, Mr Lambert sits down at the table.

"Sit down," he says to Tiffany and Max. "I want to talk to you."

Tiffany and Max are surprised, but they sit down.

"I want your help," says Mr Lambert. "There's something wrong. Owen met Marissa on an online dating site, only three months ago. Then eight weeks ago she moved to this town. Now they are getting married. Everything is happening too quickly. I don't like it. Also, Marissa will have no friends and no family at the wedding."

"Her mother will come," says Tiffany.

"Yes. But it's very strange. Marissa wants a big wedding, but her friends and family won't be there. I'm worried because we don't know anything about her."

"But Dad, you and Mom will talk to Marissa's mother, won't you? She will want to meet you. And you will want to meet her.

"Weddings are very expensive. Usually, the bride's family pays for most of the wedding," says Max.

"Not this time," says his father. "Her mother will come here two days before the wedding. Marissa says her mother doesn't like talking on the telephone. It's very strange. Marissa has no money. Owen has only a little money and he will need that when he moves to Hawaii. Marissa says her mother cannot help. Your mother wants us to pay for everything. Dresses, flowers, the wedding and the wedding party…."

Max laughs. "Oh Dad," he says. "Are you worried about the money?"

Mr Lambert is quiet for a while. Then he says slowly, "No. I'm a little angry because your mother is going crazy. So, Max, I want you to use your computer skills. You can't tell Owen what you are doing, but I want you to find out everything about Marissa. Her family name is Talbert – maybe that will help."

Max is shocked. "You are always telling me not to be a hacker!"

"I know. But something is wrong, and I want to find out what it is. Just be careful! I don't want one son in an unhappy marriage and my other son in prison!"

Tiffany is very surprised and worried. She jumps up. "We must clean the kitchen and do the dishes," she says.

When the work is finished, Tiffany and Max go back into the dining room and say goodbye.

They cycle back to Tiffany's apartment. Tiffany makes coffee.

"Are you going to do it?" she asks Max.

"Yes," says Max. "I'm not happy about it, but Dad is worried." He drinks his coffee and kisses Tiffany good night.

"See you tomorrow."

CHAPTER FOUR

The next day Tiffany and Max meet for lunch. Max looks very tired.

"Did you find out anything about Marissa?' she asks.

"No," says Max. He drinks his coke.

Tiffany waits. Max doesn't say anything.

"What did you find online?" she asks.

"Not much," says Max. "I searched all night. I didn't find any information. I looked for a Facebook page, but Marissa doesn't have one. I found the online dating site. Marissa and Owen aren't on the site anymore, but I found a way to look at the records.

"On the dating site, she said she was twenty-three years old. She grew up in San Francisco. She did a degree in drama at the University of San Francisco. Then she worked for a real estate company. Her hobbies were the same as Owen's. I guess that's how they connected.

"I looked at the records from the University of San Francisco. There was nothing about a Marissa Talbert. I wrote a program to search for Talbert/Marissa/San Francisco – I didn't get any hits."

"It's very strange," says Tiffany. "What will you do next?"

"I don't know," says Max.

Tiffany thinks. "Marissa works at BB's Car Hire. She said she was not going to work today. She is going to look at bride dresses with your mother. I don't have any classes this afternoon. I'll go to BB's. Maybe I can find out something about Marissa from her co-workers."

"How can you do that?" asks Max.

"My cousin, Lucia, also works there. I'll call you later." Tiffany takes her bag and leaves the café.

It's late afternoon before Tiffany calls Max.

"Did you find out anything about Marissa?" asks Max.

"No. She doesn't talk to anyone at work. They don't know anything. But I had an idea!" Tiffany sounds excited.

"What is it?" asks Max.

"Hmm. It's hard to explain, but please listen. One of the women in the office at BB's comes from Connecticut. Well, you know when people who come from the West coast of the USA talk, they sound a little different from people who live on the East coast of the USA."

"Yes, I know," says Max. "And we grew up in the middle of the USA, so we sound different too."

"I was listening to the woman from Connecticut, and I thought 'Marissa sounds like her!' Marissa talks like someone from the East coast. She didn't grow up in San Francisco!"

"Tiff, you're so smart!" Max is pleased. "But why didn't anyone notice?"

"Marissa said 'I come from San Francisco'. Everyone believed her, because no one was looking for a mystery," says Tiffany.

Max stands up. "I have a class now. I'm so tired. I hope I can stay awake."

"Try to stay awake," says Tiffany. "Your professor will be very angry if you sleep in his class. Can I help you search for information about Marissa?"

"Yes please. Can you come to my apartment tonight? It will be nice to be with you. You can keep me awake! Bring your laptop. I will buy hamburgers."

"OK," says Tiffany. "I will come at six thirty pm."

When Tiffany arrives at Max's apartment he says, "Good! I will order the hamburgers now. My roommate Derek is home tonight, so I will order one for him too."

Max calls the takeaway restaurant and orders hamburgers.

"I'm so tired," he says. "Let's eat first."

They talk about their classes and teachers. Tiffany is thinking about what courses to take at university next year. Max will graduate a year before Tiffany. He doesn't know what kind of job he would like.

Soon the doorbell rings. It's the hamburger delivery.

"Derek!" shouts Matt. "Dinner's here!"

Derek comes out of his bedroom. "Hi, Tiff! Good to see you. Food! Great! I'm so hungry."

Derek takes a soda from the refrigerator and sits at the dining table. He eats quickly. Then he stands up and says, "Sorry I can't stay and talk. I have a test tomorrow and I have to study."

He goes back to his bedroom.

Max and Tiffany put the hamburger boxes in the rubbish bin and clean the table. They set up their laptops on the dining table. Max connects Tiffany's laptop to the Wi-Fi.

"Now," says Tiffany. "What do you want me to do?"

Max laughs. "I plan to do some hacking. I'll be in big trouble if I get caught. You can't take any risks. But you can do some searching that is safe. Please search for telephone numbers for the name Talbert in the state of Connecticut. If you find land line numbers, you might find house addresses too."

"OK," says Tiffany.

After a while Tiffany sighs. "There are so many Talberts in Connecticut!"

"I can't find anyone called Marissa Talbert who went to university in Connecticut," says Max. "Maybe she went to university in another state. I'm going to try something else. I'm going to look at birth records."

Then he says, "A child named Marissa Talbert was born in Trammings, Connecticut, twenty-three years ago. The age is right for Owen's fiancée."

"There's a telephone number for R.G Talbert in Trammings!" Tiffany is pleased.

"A Marissa Talbert went to Trammings High School," says Max. "But it's strange. She didn't graduate. I'll look at the local newspaper. Maybe I can find an article with the name Talbert."

A few minutes later, Max says, "Oh no! Tiff! Come and look at this!"

Tiffany jumps up and walks around the table to look at the screen on Max's laptop.

She sees a newspaper article.

---Local Teenager Convicted of Dangerous Driving!

Today, eighteen-year-old Marissa Talbert was convicted of dangerous driving.

Two months ago, on the night of the Trammings High School Senior Prom,

Marissa Talbert was driving Earl Downing's car, when she drove on the wrong side of the road and hit a truck. The truck driver and Marissa Talbert were unhurt. Earl Downing died at the scene of the accident. He was eighteen years old. He was the son of Tania and Gordon Downing who are well-known residents of Trammings. His parents are in shock at the loss of their son.

Marissa Talbert has been sentenced to five years in jail for dangerous driving resulting in death.---

Tiffany and Max look at each other. "What do we do now?" asks Max.

CHAPTER FIVE

The next day Max and Tiffany meet at the student café at lunchtime. Max looks very bad. He is tired and worried. Tiffany is worried too.

"What are we going to do?" asks Max. "My father asked me to check up on Marissa. Five years ago, she was driving a car, and she killed the passenger in the car. Can I tell my father? What about Owen? He loves Marissa."

"I believe in the truth," says Tiffany. "I think you must tell your father."

"But my father will tell Owen. He will be very unhappy. I don't want to be unkind to my brother. And what about Marissa? Maybe Owen won't want to marry her."

"No. Maybe not," says Tiffany slowly. "But Marissa didn't tell Owen about her life. That's not right. If you marry someone, you should not have secrets."

Max laughs. "Marissa said you are too pretty to be a bridesmaid. So maybe you don't like her."

Tiffany is angry. "Max! Sometimes you are very stupid. You know I don't care about what Marissa said!"

"I was joking," says Max. "But help me. I don't know what to do. Shall I tell my father what I found on the Internet? Shall I tell Owen? If I tell him I hacked computer systems to find out about Marissa, he might be so angry he will never talk to me again."

Tiffany holds Max's hand. "I'm sorry. It's very difficult. I don't know what you should do."

Tiffany looks at her phone. "I'm sorry. I have to go. I have a meeting with my professor. When can we meet?"

"Tonight?" asks Max.

"OK," says Tiffany. "Come to my apartment. I'll be home after seven thirty pm. And please don't worry."

Tiffany hurries away.

Max stays in the café. He doesn't know what to do.

That night, Max goes to Tiffany's apartment. "My roommate is out on a date," says Tiffany. "So we can talk in private."

Max is still very worried, but Tiffany is cheerful.

She makes coffee and they sit in the small living room.

"I was thinking all day about the problem," she says. "My professor was annoyed with me because I wasn't listening to her. I was thinking, 'How did Marissa get a job with BB's Car Hire? If you have been in jail, it's very difficult to get a job. Some company owners will give you a second chance, but then Bob Beatty would know about Marissa's record. He's a nice guy, but he likes to gossip — I think he would tell someone. Then I thought, 'Bob Beatty is lazy'. Marissa didn't tell him about her past and he didn't check up on her."

Max says, "But how does that help us?"

"It doesn't help us. But I thought about how I didn't like her very much when we first met. But now I feel sorry for her. I think she worries all the time that someone will find out about her past. I think her life is very difficult. So I had an idea."

Max drinks some coffee and looks at Tiffany. He loves her, but sometimes her mind is too quick for him. He doesn't know where her thoughts are going.

"What's your idea, Tiff?"

Tiffany laughs. "It's easy! We talk to Marissa. She is lonely and frightened. I think her secret is so big that she might want to tell someone. So maybe she will tell us!"

"OK," says Max slowly. "When will we talk to her?"

"Here! Tonight! She should be here soon."

"How did you that?" asks Max.

"I called your mother and said, 'I want to talk to Marissa about a wedding present'. She gave me Marissa's phone number."

Tiffany picks up her phone. "Then I texted her." Tiffany reads from her message log. "I wrote --- *I'm your friend. I don't want anything bad to happen to you, but I want to talk to you. Please come to my apartment tonight. The address is two three seven A College Avenue'---.''*

"But Tiff! She won't come!"

"I think she will."

"Tiff! Don't tell her I hacked the university records! Don't tell her anything we know."

"Trust me. We won't have to."

Max is shaking his head when the doorbell rings. Tiffany goes to open the door. It's Marissa. Tiffany hugs her. "Come in."

Marissa comes into the living room. She sees Max. "What is he doing here?" she shouts.

Tiffany pats Marissa's arm. "It's OK. Sit down."

Marissa sits on the sofa. She looks very unhappy.

"What do you want?" she asks.

"We don't want anything, but we are worried about you. We think you need to talk to us," says Tiffany.

"Why?' asks Marissa.

"We think you have a secret. We think your life story is different from what you told Owen. We want to help."

Marissa's face is red. She starts crying. "How did you know I have a secret?"

Max is very worried. What is Tiff going to say?

"We know from the way you talk that you didn't grow up on the West coast of the USA. You grew up on the East coast, didn't you? And you want a big wedding, but only your mother will come. No friends or other family – something is wrong. Why don't you tell us your secret?"

"But you'll tell everyone. You'll tell Owen and his parents. I love Owen. I want to marry him. I want to go to Hawaii with him!" Marissa is shouting again.

"We won't tell anyone. We want to help," says Tiffany.

Max says, "Owen loves you. We want you both to be happy. I promise you Tiff and I will never tell anyone what you tell us."

Marissa sighs. "I have been so lonely. Then I met Owen. It was like a dream, but I am never happy, because of my past. I will tell you my story."

CHAPTER SIX

"I grew up in a very small town in Connecticut. It is called Trammings. My father had a hardware store. He rented the building from the Downing family. They own everything in the town. They are very rich. Mr and Mrs Downing had a son called Earl. He was very good-looking and very charming. Everyone in the town liked him. I didn't like him. I always thought he wasn't a nice person. The high school in my hometown was very small. Earl was the most popular boy in the school. He was in the same year as me.

"In our senior year, he asked me to the prom. I was very surprised. There were many girls in our school year who were much prettier than me. I wanted to say 'no'. But my father said 'Go to the prom with Earl – it will be good for my business. You will be popular. My sister agreed with him. 'Wow,' she said. 'You must say 'yes'. My mother didn't say anything. I think she didn't like Earl either. I went to the prom with him. I didn't have a good time. He danced with the other girls. Then I saw that he had a small bottle of vodka in his pocket. He was drinking all the time.

"When the prom finished, we went out to his car. I said, 'You have been drinking. You cannot drive.'

He said, 'I'm OK', but he was so drunk, he dropped his car keys on the ground. I picked them up. I said, 'I'll drive you to your house. Then I'll call my father. He'll come and take me home.'

He couldn't say anything, because I had his car keys. We got in the car, and I drove towards his parents' house. Then he said, 'Let's go to the forest! We will have a good time!'

"I said 'No! I want to go home.' 'Yes! Yes!' he said. He pulled on the steering wheel. The car ran across the road. There was a truck coming the other way. The car hit the truck. Earl was killed. But I was OK.

"No one believed my story. Earl's family were so powerful. They said, 'That girl killed our son. She is a killer.'

"The blood tests showed that Earl had drunk a lot of alcohol. There was no alcohol in my blood. But the police chief was frightened of the Downing family. They said, 'Marissa killed our beautiful boy. She is nobody. Her father only has a hardware store.'

"Maybe the family paid the police chief a lot of money. I don't know. But I was sent to prison for five years! My father lost his hardware shop. My sister hates me. She says I destroyed her life. My cousins and friends hate me too. The only person who believed me was my mother.

"I got out of prison after three years. When I came out of prison, my mother said, 'You can't come back to this town. You must make a new life.' My parole officer agreed I could not go back to Trammings. She helped me to make a new life in San Francisco. But I was lonely. I wanted a boyfriend. So after a while, I joined the dating service and met Owen.

"Maybe you think I'm selfish, but I love Owen. And all my life I dreamt of my wedding. But now my parents are poor, and my father won't talk to me. I lost everything. I want to have Owen, and I want a wedding!"

<h1 style="text-align:center">CHAPTER SEVEN</h1>

Marissa stops talking. Tiffany and Max don't say anything.

"You don't believe me! Nobody believes me!" Marissa cries and cries.

Tiffany sits next to her of the sofa and hugs her. "I believe you. I believe every word you said. I'm so sorry you had such a bad time," she says.

"What about Max?" asks Marissa.

"I believe you too," he says.

I'm going to make more coffee," says Tiffany. "We have to make a plan. We have to decide what we are going to do."

"What do you mean?" shouts Marissa. "No one can do anything. And you said, 'I won't tell anyone'."

Tiffany makes coffee. Marissa is sitting on the sofa crying.

"Marissa," says Max quietly. "You have to tell Owen everything."

"No! He won't love me anymore."

"That's not true. He loves you. He'll believe you," says Max. "You want to be happy. You'll never be happy if you have such a big secret."

"I'm scared," says Marissa. Her hands are shaking. Tiffany takes the coffee cup out of Marissa's hands and puts it on the table. She hugs her again. "Of course you are scared. But if you love Owen, you will tell him."

"OK," says Marissa slowly.

Max looks at his phone. "It's nine pm. Where is Owen tonight?"

"He said he was working late. But I'm sure he's finished now," says Marissa.

"OK," says Max. "Call him. Tell him to come here."

"Now?" Marissa looks very scared.

"Yes," says Max. "Do it!"

Marissa calls Owen. "I'm at Tiffany's apartment," she says. "Can you come here? I have something I want to tell you."

After a few seconds, she hangs up. She looks at Max and Tiffany. "He was surprised, but he says he will be here in ten minutes."

"Don't worry," says Max. "You know you have to tell him. I promise you it will be OK."

The three young people sit in silence until the doorbell rings. Tiffany answers the door.

"Come in Owen," she says. "Max and I are going out for coffee. Call us when you and Marissa have finished talking."

Max and Tiffany go to a bar. "I know you don't like to drink a lot," says Max. "But I have had so much coffee and I'm very nervous. I need a beer!"

Tiffany asks for a glass of white wine. They sit at a small table in a corner. "Did we do the right thing?" asks Max.

Tiffany looks worried. "I hope so. But we had to do something. We couldn't tell anyone. I think this is the best way."

They sit in the bar and wait for Owen to call Max. They don't talk. They are too worried. Max finishes one beer, and buys another one.

Finally, Owen calls. Max puts his phone on speaker. Tiffany leans towards the phone to listen.

"Hi Owen," says Max. "Is everything OK?"

"Come back here now!" says Owen and hangs up.

They hurry back to Tiffany's apartment. They are both very, very worried.

Outside the door, they look at each other. Max takes a big breath and opens the door. Owen and Marissa are sitting on the sofa. They are both smiling. Marissa looks very happy.

"Thank you, Bro and Tiffany," says Owen. "Everything is very OK."

"I feel so much better," says Marissa. "It was so bad when I was keeping secrets from Owen. Thank you!"

She jumps up and hugs Max and Tiffany. Owen hugs them too.

They all sit down. Owen says, "We will tell Mom and Dad about what happened to Marissa, but no one else. Do you agree?"

"Of course," say Max and Tiffany. "We will never say anything."

Especially about all the illegal hacking I did to find out about Marissa's past, thinks Max.

Marissa and Owen talk and talk about their plans for the future. It's late and Tiffany is yawning, so everyone else leaves. At the door, Marissa says, "And please be my bridesmaid."

"But Tonia will be your bridesmaid," says Tiffany quickly.

Max laughs. "What's the joke?" asks Owen.

"Tiffany doesn't like being a bridesmaid. She says the dresses are always ugly," laughs Max.

"I can have two bridesmaids," says Marissa. She looks very happy. "I chose a dress for Tonia, but you can wear any dress you like."

"Mom won't like that," says Owen. "The bridesmaids always have the same dresses."

"Not at our wedding," laughs Marissa.

CHAPTER EIGHT

The next day, Max gets a text from Owen.

---Marissa and I will go and talk to Mom and Dad tonight. Wish us luck.---

Max is not worried. He answers, *---Our parents know that bad things can happen in small towns. Especially when there is a rich and powerful family who can put pressure on the police. It will be OK.---*

Late that night he gets a message from Owen. It is a smiley emoji.

Max's Dad calls him. "Thank you. I knew there was something wrong. Now I know Marissa's story, everything is fine."

"But I had to do some hacking to get the answers! You always tell me not to do it!" laughs Max.

"Yes, I know. But this time it was the right thing to do. And please thank Tiffany too. She's a very clever young woman with a big heart!"

Marissa's mother comes from Connecticut. She's a very nice women and Owen and Max's mother likes her very much. They talk a lot and are very excited.

The wedding is wonderful. The bride is beautiful. Tiffany wears a dress that is the same colour as Tonia's. Max gets a haircut and looks very handsome in his tuxedo.

The bride and groom won't have a honeymoon because they have to leave for Hawaii.

"But beautiful Hawaii will be a long, long honeymoon for us," says Owen.

When everyone is leaving after the wedding party, Marissa and Owen come to talk to Max and Tiffany.

"Thank you so much," they say. "We will have a happy marriage because of what you did."

"You're welcome", say Tiffany and Max.

THANK YOU

Thank you for reading Tiffany and Max Solve a Mystery (Word count: 5,390) We hope you enjoyed it.

There is another book in the Tiffany and Max series:
Tiffany and Max Investigate

If you would like to read more graded readers, please visit our website http://www.italkyoutalk.com

Other Level 2 graded readers include
Adventure in Rome
Andre's Dream
A New Life
A Passion for Music
Christmas Tales
Danger in Seattle
Don't Come Back
Dressed for Success
Elspeth and the Visitor
Finders Keepers…
How Did You Meet?
Hunted in Hong Kong
John Sees a Murder
Made by Minty

Marcy's Bakery
Men's Konkatsu Tales
Message in a Bottle
Murder in Marrakech
Murder on Whale Island
Neighbours
Salaryman Secrets!
Stories for Halloween
The Cruise Ship
The Perfect Wedding
The House in the Forest
The Kindness of Strangers
The School on Bolt Street
The Secret Door
Train Travel
Trouble in Paris
Who's There?
Women's Konkatsu Tales

ABOUT THE AUTHOR

I Talk You Talk Press is an award-winning Japan-based publisher of language textbooks, graded readers and language learning/teaching resources. We won the Language Learner Literature Award in 2019 and 2020.

Our team is made up of highly experienced language teachers and translators, who have all studied at least one additional language to an advanced level.

This experience enables us to design our materials from the perspective of both the teacher and the learner. We consult with both teachers and language learners when designing our textbooks and graded readers, and test our materials extensively in the classroom before publication.

We are a fast-growing press, and currently publish graded readers for learners of English. We publish new graded readers monthly.